WET PAINT

A Poetry Storm

Rhae Angela Tomeoni

POWER TRIP PRESS

Published by Power Trip Press

Cover & Book design : Mokey's Village

Author Contact : MokeysVillage@rocketmail.com

Library of Congress Txu 1 -308-724

First Edition

ISBN 978-0-615-74595-4

-THE ORDER-

appreciations -

bob & martha - parents living in heaven

gregory -   husband   (the one)
cajun   -   daughter
emio   -   son
vicki   -   cousin

terris mike murphy   - for pushing me off the cliff
"my-tai" (malia)   - for editing   (my niece)
gracious listeners   - you know who you are
*   - from New York to California*

'tony dubovsky, max cooperstein, emio, cajun & vicki for the
combined gifts of artwork, photos, drawings. You gave my
story a heartbeat.*

**super special thanks to ANTHONY DUBOVSKY, an esteemed
California artist, for the honor of allowing me to associate
his drawings with my poems at my discretion, bringing forth
new meaning neither of us could ever have imagined.*

- because I write -

-angela-

I define my poetry as "soul food." My writing style continues to evolve with the lessons of time, be it in love's <u>heat</u> or the <u>chill</u> of devastating loss.

Extracting from these mountain top awakenings, diverting a bit from the mainstream, my style seems to take on its own configuration.

My objective: Perhaps ultimately to redeem my hope. By expressing vast rainbows of emotions, striving to connect the "dots" of Life's Grand Tour through words...   I am able to maintain balance, though the earth undulates beneath me.

Rhae Angela Tomeoni
         of
Berkeley, California

The Storm

EPISODE ONE

I FELL IN LOVE - everything is
p e r f e c t . . . .
confused newlyweds
                    playing house
                    raising children
GRANDPA - GRANDMA

                    nothing but LOVE

I HAD NO IDEA . . .

about love, you know, the kind in fairy tales . . .

the kind in forbidden gardens of joy . . .

the kind you dreamed of as a child in blossom . . .

the kind you fantasized about, creating a world

     of make-believe more real than touch . . .

the kind that lets you see crystal night stars

        in the blue sky of day . . .

Until you said hello

      I HAD NO IDEA

SOMEDAY

Someday I'll write a poem about my mother . . .

but I'm not sure how it would begin . . .
she's all the woman I could ever hope to be
. . . I admire her . . .

she's a small lady, when she loses an ounce
she gets too skinny

       but she's the biggest mom I'll ever have . . .

DAMN! I really want to write a poem about her
               but what would I say?

she is a totally lovely person in ways
           surely, I have yet to see . . .

she's been my mom for 28 years now . . .

she hasn't changed much . . . her smile, still
big as ever . . . her touch still feels secure . . .
her laugh still makes me rejoice . . . she
manages to spread herself among many, yet
when I need her full attention -
           I am not denied . . .

I LOVE this woman selfishly, because

what we have is special, warm and kind ... it's OURS!

I like it 'cause no one can enter our world . . .

Someday, yeah, I think I'll write that poem . . .

THERE IS THIS MAN WHO LOOKS FAMILIAR

HE'S BEEN AROUND ME ALL MY LIFE
I THINK HE HAS SOME GROWN UP KIDS
I KNOW HE HAS A WIFE

HE DRIVES A LITTLE SPORTS CAR
IT SEEMS TO FIT HIS STYLE

I BET IF IT GOT WRECKED
HE'D BE SICK FOR QUITE A WHILE

WELL HE SEEMS KIND AS EVER
BUT I WONDER WHO HE IS

ONE DAY I'M GOING TO FOLLOW HIM
AND FIND OUT WHERE HE LIVES

I KNOW I'LL FIND THE HOUSE
FEELS VERY MUCH LIKE HOME

'CAUSE THIS MAN'S MY DADDY
SO I NEVER AM ALONE

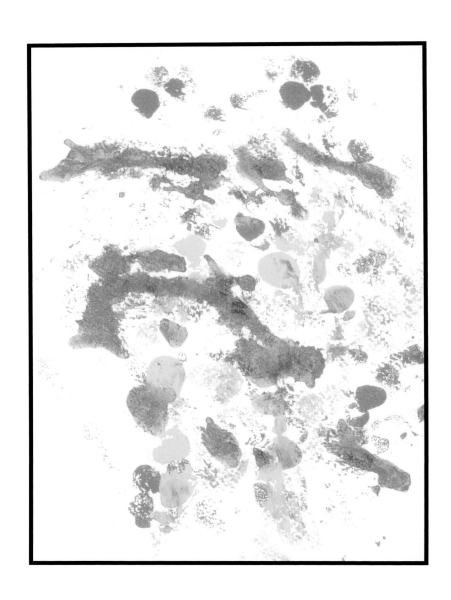

SOMETHING BEAUTIFUL HAS HAPPENED

For me a niece, an auntie I have become . . .
For my mother, a grandaughter to fill her
already abundant heart . . .
For my papa, a new reason to quiver his chin,
grandpa he can now be called . . .

For my younger brother, with uncle before his
name, somehow no longer seems so young . . .

The greatest pride of all goes to my BIG brother
for the welcomed arrival of his precious baby girl . . .

and the radiant proud mother....who brightened this world
with a daughter of her very own....

My heart is bursting with joy . . .
        I am so proud of my family . . .

ARE YOU GONNA BE OK TODAY ?

I WORRY WHEN YOU FROWN, YOUR RATHER LARGE EXPRESSIVE EYES
SEEM TROUBLED WHEN FIRST THEY GREET THE LIGHT OF DAY.

I AM UNEASY WHEN YOUR APPARENT FRUSTRATION SURFACES, LIKE
RESTLESS WIND BLOWING LEAVES FROM AN AUTUMN TREE.

i saw you yesterday, like a stone wall braced for the abuses of this harsh
world . . . i have
seen the wall crumble in graceful awkwardness
                    shattered in illusion . . .

I HAVE SEEN CALM . . . in you i have witnessed chaos

i have seen you elated . . . I HAVE SEEN YOU
                                DEGRADED

i have kissed virgin tears from your eyes . . .

I AM SO DEEPLY MOVED WITH INSUPPRESSIBLE
CONCERN FOR YOU

                        the words no longer flow
                          i am shaking

            therefore I close

yet wondering . .

                    ARE YOU GONNA BE OK TODAY . . . ?

BLACK GIRL

Your beauty surfaces more everyday . . .

I feel closer to you in so many ways . . .

Having you around has been a blessing
                          in my world . . .

I don't know what I'd do without you
                          stay close to me girl . . .

A few times in my life I had little to have pride in . . .

When I looked around I found you to confide in . . .

I know we are related, our moms are close too, if not for blood

                          I would still cling to you . . .

You know who you are
          but for those who do not . . .

     SHE'S MY COUSIN VICKI . . . I love her a lot . . .

-WITH YOU-

During the day when we are apart, your powerful
image flashes across my mind's eye, effortlessly
I submit to a child-like anxiousness.

Fulfill my fondest dream, your smile, your
touch, your love.

If an angel took my hand, lead me on a flight
through heaven, I would return comparing it to
knowing you.

If happiness resembled the dancing tail
of a mercury colored kite, riding high,
I could point up and say, "hey! look at
me inside."

Through all our endeavors, in respect of those
yet in creation, I can say that nothing has
been lost for me.

WITH YOU.. I have tasted pure gladness and bathed in
peace untampered.

WITH YOU.. I have cried in joy, 'til laughter resounds.

WITH YOU.. my heart rings like distant church bells
in the night.

Enchantment is mine when I am WITH YOU.

IN MY ESTIMATION . . .

    A portrait of your smiling face

        should be hung right next to the moon . . .

_____

YOU KNOW . . . I COULD BE JEALOUS OF THE WIND . . .

    FOR IT CARESSES YOU GENTLY . . .

in my estimation . . .

~ *dream maker* ~

wishing is wanting and wanting is you and you

are precious and precious is rare and rare is

special and special is tempting and tempting is

desire and desire is strong and strong is binding

and binding is lasting and lasting is forever and

forever is eternal and eternal is life and life

is beautiful and beautiful is you and you are

a dream......... my dream which came true........

EPISODE TWO

Shattered Reality

the " *grim reaper* " comes to get my family! Grandmother, Father, Aunt, many wonderful Friends but was "generous" enough to leave me my MOTHER

A Promise

the news is bad

my father . . . my source of encouragement . . . a dependable
valley of understanding . . . the first man I loved

my father . . . now upon himself wishing for a way out, a
deep sad burning to live . . . no more

but . . . well . . . hey . . . what about the child in him,
the adventuresome little boy of six ?
"come on in son, it's raiiiiining ." . . . .
         wanting so to continue his fantasies . . . frolicking
in the damp grass . . . . "oh please can I stay out....
let me stay . . . . . a while longer?"

or the big kid of 17 . . . bursting with the urgency to
prove himself a man

the father of three beautiful . . . hmmm children . . .
. . . . now with children . . . .

his grandaughter, only three months old . . . tell me, is the
suffering of the mind and soul so overbearing that he cannot
wait to hear her first unmistakable . . . hello   ? ? ?

yes . . . the news is bad

i walk   trance-like through the crowd at noon . . .
tears streaking my face . . . vision blurred . . . eyes stinging

people, noise, colors   all a mass of nothingness

in the midst . . . a flicker of light . . . sparkling warmth
and understanding . . . a reason to dry my sorrows

                 a promise_____ YOU ____

A Promise Part II
(years later)

The trouble with collecting things is –

finding the one thing you didn't need to find at the time you found it –

digging through a pile of odds and ends –– AKA the junk drawer, searching for

some blue thread, I ran across a painful memory –– a poem I wrote about my

father before he ended his life –– I froze –– read it ––

choked up so badly –– But it's Thanksgiving Day –– Really it is ––

Why , you may wonder... because life had become very difficult following his
stroke...handicapped, dependent, fear gripping his every moment...

HIS CHOICE

I miss you daddy

pg13

Precious Memories

Good morning Lord
I have something on my mind
I wonder would you help me one more time.
I have a friend who is dear to my heart,
who is nearing the time with this life he must part.
Oh Lord, would you bless not once but twice,
Keep his family in your care for the rest of their lives.
He is precious, he is an anchor, he is the one we adore.
Oh Lord, if you would, please bless him once more.
He is faithful, he is a teacher, he is our gift from above.
Oh Lord, would you wrap him all up in your love.
Give him comfort, give him peace,
make his journey so sweet.
We will miss him so deeply – our lives he made complete.
We are proud of him and we thank you for
keeping him in your will.
He's the sunrise, the sunset, he's a light on the hill.
Lord we're thankful and forever grateful
for the grace you have shown.
We were infants – then elders, in your love we have grown.
Your understanding your forgiveness , so infinite, we are in awe.
We are humbled by the good in each of us you saw.
You pick us up when we fall,
You answer when we call,
For everything Lord, we love you,
And again I must say,
Good morning Lord,
Have a beautiful day.

MAY I HAVE YOUR ATTENTION PLEASE . . .

I would like to make an announcement . . .

Angels have been traveling through

like a sweet Sunday morning breeze

weaving intricate patterns using fine threads of gold

marking their passage with perfect filigreed moments

etched in our hearts forever

loving memory – friend

a love story

many years ago a little boy named emio went to school. there must have been something special about him, having attracted the amoré of one smiling, friendly, warm, loving cafeteria lady named "willy".

maybe it was his extremely long double-decker eyelashes, swooping over his huge brown eyes. maybe it was his demeanor - self assured and innocent.

she took him under her wing and became his ally in a world of new experiences. he was five and life at school had begun.

"willy", through her ways, had discovered he didn't like fish. friday was fish day for cafeteria lunch. she started making him bologna sandwiches to ensure her little emio was happy. bologna sandwiches escalated into his own private delivery of BBQ. i said, " 'willy', you're spoiling him rotten" - she replied " i know but i love that little boy." everyday she looked for him so she could laugh inside at his funny walk.

We stayed in touch throughout the years. So once again stopping on our way home, i proudly brought the now 15 year-old mustache-sporting, 5'9" basketball player in to see her   .... looking up, tears in her eyes, smiling, she asked him, "emio, you still like bologna sandwiches?"
        he laughed... warmly they embraced.... for the last time....

emio is of mixed heritage. i, his mom, black ; his dad, italian. he was named in memory of my husband's father emio——in italian meaning "he's mine".............."WILLY", EMIO IS YOURS

loving memory friend

A Stitch - n - Time

Dressmaker, Dressmaker – you are losing your skill
Your hands have been blessed, they still have their will
The stitch that is missing is the control of your mind
It is having great difficulty stitching in time
One stitch goes left, one goes right
You now have been stitching 'til late into night
It is painful to watch your craft lose its edge
anxious you become but determination you pledge
kings and queens – you have adorned
Now your garments are uneven – sometimes torn
You cannot see it while keeping your pace
But time is winning – you are losing the race
Stitch up or stitch down – you can be certain of this
God blessed you richly .....when he gave you this gift .....

Loving Memory – Relative

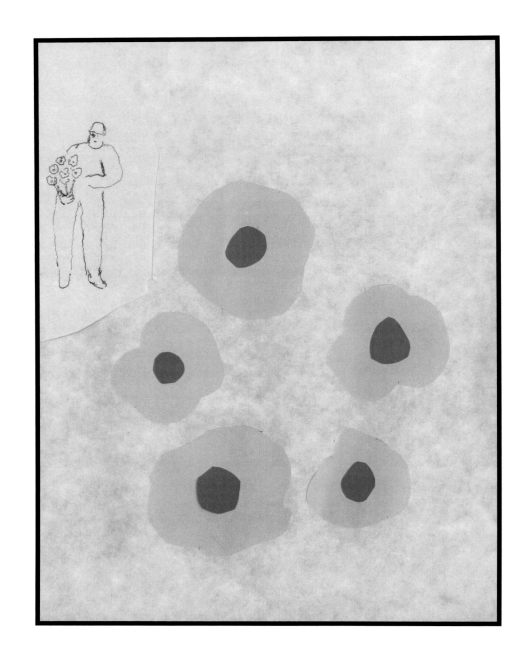

EPISODE THREE

5 minutes
In
Wonderland

In Wonderland

Please leave me a message
'cuz I ain't home -
I took a mental vacation
gonna' let my mind roam.

Tell me all the urgent stuff
which hurts my head -
When I get back I'll listen
to what you said.

For a few hours of quiet
and freedom to dream -
I will set sail for months -
at least to me it will seem.

Check in with me later
after a postcard or two
I'm away being healthy
with so much to do.

I'm relaxing my shoulders
breathing deeper than ever -
enjoying the daydream
coupled with perfect weather.

When evening comes and
you've yet to hear from me -
be proud for I've learned
the art of being free.

Please, leave me a message
I'll respond in due time -
For now, I'm a mind-drifter

.... doing just fine..............

pg19

Hush Clock

Hush Clock - your ticking is
distracting me while I'm
trying to concentrate -

Hush clock - please I ask -
your beat is yours, not mine -

Hush clock - your rhythm pushes
me forward - I want to
stay back -

Hush clock - your hands and
face are changing -
I rather enjoy still images -

Hush clock - tick tock tick tock
you're permeating my thoughts -

Hush clock - you're pulling
me in and I'm getting
weary -

Oh clock you had to have
it your way -

AND NOW I'M STUCK !
abiding by your rules -
moving forward -
moving on -
getting wiser -
getting strong -
under a shady tree - reflecting   .... hush clock....

YOU LEFT SOMETHING

an unexpected knock at the door...not ready for the day much less company
I yelled out "who is it, please" a soft sweet voice replies "me"

despite the fact that my teeth had not been brushed, I whisked open the door to the blazing morning sun, blinding my initial vision

there you are, my sad pretty cousin, 13 years my junior, but oh so grown up at 41
struggling with life's complicated issues, you chose to greet me in teary need

SOME TWO HOURS LATER...

you unveiled your inner beauty through talk, tears, and a very runny nose, upon leaving, we embraced once more . . . you drove away blowing kisses, feeling better

me, now feeling more maternal than ever, though I've grown kids of my own, walked slowly across the brick-tiled hallway, into my newly carpeted living room

briefly glancing back at the door of intrigue, pausing to look down I noticed that......

YOU LEFT SOMETHING....three teardrops...which involuntarily ran down your face, to your chin, dripping on the tiled floor...

three beautiful teardrops which I will let dry naturally............

NEW YORK SURPRISE

Two happy faces-

ONE the grateful and proud recipient of a new
pink cowboy hat with a shoestring yellow bow

sitting atop the head of a happy face ...

TWO a dirty homeless guy with twinkling bright
white eyes, a couple of teeth, the grateful and

proud recipient of my leftover hot dinner

utensils and napkin included...

"*He*" came back to get my mom

Grief-stricken the process

begins

Dreams - thoughts -poems - rivers - valleys - mountains

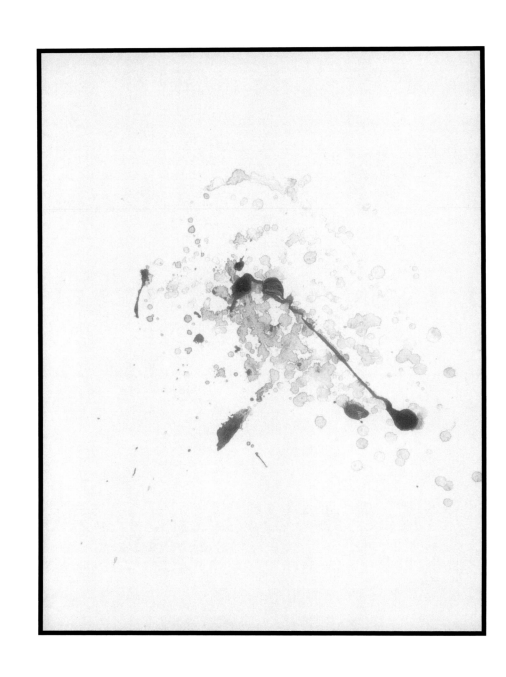

FULL IMPACT

the target—my soul
the weapon —a wrecking ball strapped to a towering crane in the sky
the motion   —increasing with every swing
the power   —increasing with every sway

eyes closed—teeth clenched—fists balled,
bracing myself for the impact
brow soaked with trembling beads of sweat
heart pounding so loud 'til ears no longer hear
ass so tight—the jaws of life could not pry it apart

COULD YOU IMAGINE!!!

MOMMY DIED—right before my eyes

sing to me mommy...smile for me mommy...laugh with me mommy....

PLEASE.....I'm standing here right beside you...

FULL IMPACT   **mommy died**

the wrecking ball struck its target........**ME !**

Cancer! You Filthy Thief

Cancer you filthy thief – you creeped in taking up residence
while we were on a dream vacation – you picked the locks of our
hearts – entered our domain – you even had the nerve to redecorate
our home sweet home – you invaded our private treasures – you
stole the rubies and emeralds from our family jewelry box – you read
our diary – you impressed yourself in our sturdy mirror staring at
your ugly distorted face you grinned – repeatedly you made hostile
phone calls and left us the bill – I despise you cancer – yet –
because you are so crafty so silent so smooth – I stand in raw disdain
– never do I want to shake your sweaty hand – you overstayed
your invasion - you knew we would be home soon – we were so happy
so free until we stood at the threshold of home – bags still packed -
pictures undeveloped – gifts undelivered – during the twinkling of
holiday decorations – the aroma of honey-cloved ham – you
dimmed the lights, while consuming our feast – POOF! Be gone – you
are not my friend nor my fondest memory – in fact you are loathed
by my brain, I suffocate you from my thoughts - see how you like it...
Vanish! like the DIRT that you are back to HELL from whence you
came . . .

my mother-

my queen -

an innocent victim

of pancreatic cancer-

Her Eyes -
     You ask me why – why do I miss you -
     because your eyes answered my unasked questions –
     because your eyes saw through my struggles -
     because your eyes gave me assurance –
          when words became tainted with falsehood –

     because your eyes called out my name – before you parted your
               lips to speak –
     because your eyes showered me with sparkly things –
               you know, fairy dust -
     because how I walked and moved was orchestrated by your eyes –

     picky, critical, encouraging, tenderly shaping your creation
     with all the confidence and pride a mother is due -

Mother – you ask me why – why do I miss you so –
     because my eyes can't see your eyes anymore –
          I do not know how to see things on my own –
               because your eyes called out my name -
                    before you parted your lips to speak -

BECAUSE

Because of what she gave me
I am able to <u>stand</u> supported
by her never failing love – her
uncanny way of stretching
threads of kisses & hugs to me
no matter where in this world
I may have been

Because of what she gave me
my dreams are to ride the cloud
      that absorbs the sound of the midnight train . . . .

Because of what she gave me
I am strong also confident
I can swim up river - I
can dry the tear of a weeping
child – sprinkle a bit of humor
in my hand - blow it like feathers
bringing a smile to a
little sad face

Because of what she gave me
I listen to the early bird sing
finding myself searching the
sky or tree to verify that this
little bird is singing
just for me

Because of what she gave me
FOREVER will I feel her heart beating
deeply inside of mine

     hers..mine..hers..mine..

The Woman Who Embraced Me –

here come the tears again
and I am stranded

stranded in a moment of
deep yearning for the touch
of my mother – a touch never
to be felt on this earth again
a touch reaffirming
my right to happiness and
security   . . . . when to my amazement. . . .

a woman embraced me, enabling me to finish shopping,
make it home and sit down!

The LETTER
&
three poems
from my Mom

The Letter

On the threshhold of a new adventure, the biggest and most important of my life. I learned two days ago that I, (hard to write this) have cancer of the pancreas and it is inoperable.

First reaction: tremendous concern for my kids- how will they handle this knowledge, especially my daughter (we're so close).

Devastating as it is I'm not as overwhelmed as I could be, perhaps because it came without warning, took me by surprise . However, whatever the case may be , I'm alright and I believe if I can face this bravely my kids and other loved ones will keep strong.

Some of my thoughts: Initially sadness not being here to see how my grandchildren turn out. I have such high hopes for them, but on the other hand I have had a glimpse of their potential .

-my mom

IF THERE

We're told that somewhere out there beyond
time and space - if there is a place somewhere
that friends and loved ones meet -

I'm sure you'll have a warm reception
as you walk down the street -

Because it seems as though the last one out -
    forgot - to shut the door

       -My Mom

MEMORIES

Stored in unlikely places
     floating in the kitchen
when it's supper time
     Sometimes they're hidden in the
unidentifiable flavor of a candy jelly bean —
     taste of a long forgotten sweet
But they send your thoughts running back
     to some place or time in childhood

       -My Mom

SOLDIER

Life's weapons seem
     unduly cruel, unfair
and so strong - they chipped
     away my exterior but
never touched my spirit —
     This soldier fought valiantly

       - My Mom

EPISODE SIX

Cajun's Pages

SHE.......

She crawled, she struggled, she pulled, she craved, holding on
'til she stood

She focused, she waddled, she hoped, never giving in
'til she walked

She dreamed, she envisioned, she believed 'til she ran – in sheer ecstasy
'til she almost flew – – –

Unaware of the red ball, rolling haplessly in her path

She tripped, she fell, she was hurt and bleeding, "MOMMY" she cried out
I was her safehouse – her instinctive source of comfort and well-being,
I was her safehouse

She crawled, she struggled, she pulled, she craved, holding on
'til she completed elementary school

She focused, she waddled, she hoped, never giving in
'til she graduated from high school

She dreamed, she envisioned, she believed 'til she went to college – in sheer
ecstasy 'til she almost flew ---

Unaware of the mental illness rolling haplessly in her path

She tripped, she fell, she is hurt and bleeding, "MOMMY" she no longer cried out
I am no longer her safehouse – no longer her instinctive, source of comfort and
well-being , I was her safehouse

NO!

Mental illness you did not give birth to her !
Mental illness you did not nurture her!
Mental illness you are not her hero! I AM!

I AM!   HER SAFEHOUSE!

pg33

WRINKLES

THE WRINKLES IN MY HUSBAND'S WASHED BUT UN-IRONED SHIRTS
GROW DEEPER AS THE PILE OF SHIRTS INCREASES.

THE WRINKLES IN MY FACE, THOUGH BARELY THERE, YET NOTICABLE TO
MY RELENTLESS INSPECTING GLARE, GROW DEEPER AS THE PILE
OF UN-IRONED SHIRTS BECOMES MY TASK.

THE WRINKLES ON MY 22 YEAR-OLD DAUGHTER'S PILLOW BECOME
EXTENSIONS OF HER FACE AS SHE LAYS ON HER BACK, INNOCENTLY
BLOWING BUBBLES FROM HER BUBBLE BOTTLE.

       I WOULD LOVE TO BLOW BUBBLES-

I WOULD LOVE HER TO IRON-

       SHE IS MENTALLY ILL-

       I AM TIRED-

Things I've Counted

With sun-warmed shoulders
sitting with knees tucked under my chin
on splintered back porch stairs

With the sweet smell of orange and lemon trees
intermingled with wild mint leaves
filling my lungs to bursting

Safely, I count the doves' call - coo ca-coo coo coo
(I was five)

Not one, not two, not three, not four
not five, not six, not seven, not eight but nine
times I've counted - a close friend or family member has
gone... gone to that... secret place
five of those times I witnessed,
I listened, I kissed, I consoled, I prayed

Things I've counted

The days each passing - wondering when
the pain, sorrow, loneliness and
torment of my daughter's mental illness will subside
just enough so that she too can ......

Safely - - - sit with sun-warmed shoulders

and count the doves' call - - - coo ca-coo coo coo

(now I'm fifty)

THEE OCCASION

onshore winds rolling in - cool yet surprisingly warm..
not in the nature of a tropical breeze nor an ensuing
hurricane..more like rhythmic breathing..sweet and low..

from such a distance you have come..depths within your gentle
body's aching soul..YOU, OH CAJUN..have risen above thee
...touching the stars...
embracing the light of their twinkling...reaching into the
"somewhere".... YOU, OH CAJUN... dipped your hands into the
"pot of gold" running nimbly back over the RAINBOW

rise above thee - OH CAJUN

EPISODE SEVEN

emio's pages

DARK AND LOVELY

we stood at the evening window... sharing an unforgettable vision of beauty...the impressive contrast of the full moon resting confidently against the vast starless black sky...

I remarking, "isn't it lovely, so dark and lovely"   *HE, in equal contrast ... his double-lashed plush wide eyes gazing up at me, repeating in breathless wonder... "YES, dark and lovely just like you ... mommy"*

he was only five years old............

PURE HEART

Who is this HEART who commands your attention ... who rises to the top of the most challenging occasions ?

Who is this HEART who commands your attention ... despite the mountain's magnitude, rises repeatedly, to the top of the most challenging occasions ?

Who is this HEART, when life seems all consuming ... breaks through with a gift of healing words, purity and strength ... seemingly grabbing the second hand ... crushing the moment that hurts so badly ?

Who is this HEART whose years are on the underside of 20.... brimming with wisdom on the overside of 80 ?

My bedroom door, cracked open enough for him to have heard me weeping.. says to me ....   "YES ,CRY – BUT NEVER IN THE DARK" .....WHO?

my son named <u>EMIO</u>

THE MAN

he has wings hidden beneath his pin striped suit

he can fly at will and post himself atop the empire state
momentarily to give "that moon" a wink

suddenly soaring with circus-like agility over autumn's
golden gate

         landing on a sunny-sunday california beach in
stylish new york shoes

     bearing gifts and great stories...... he izzz home for a
visit..........

same boyish grin, same double decker eyelashes, same
crazy kid... now flies across country stopping in to stock up
on some much needed family love....
       ...all grown up....

           my my..........

EPISODE EIGHT

fun and healing

TIME-BALM

Having been placed on the frontline with no weapons of <u>war</u>!
Sent to fight the battle of my life - with my bare hands - bleeding, blistered,
worn and ragged - I now grant myself permission to heal -

Applying the soothing, healing balm of time - I now fill the cracks in my palms -
sores on my soul - pain in my memory - with the blessings of each and every
new day -

AMEN!

Laughing From Funny Places

Around the corner of so many memories
on the day of my mother's birth –
today, yes, her birthday - I manage to laugh.

Not teenage giggle –
not hoot and holler – not unto tears
not in ecstasy – not in pivotal pain
not in the abyss of sorrow's pit –
certainly not because of what was said.

Because of time - the passage –
the extreme, profound rocket ship,
head spinning, neck wrenching,
jaw dropping movement of time!

      Yes, I laugh from funny places
          memories – and sharing memories
               makes me laugh from funny places.

ODE TO THE FUNNY TRINKET

The things I would not
buy.. you know, the old
lady yard sale stuff..
the laced table runner
with the embroidered
bumble bees on the
ends.

You know, the ceramic
flower basket with the
hummingbird painted
on the left corner...

You know, the discount
stuff "all that
glitters is not gold"
kinda stuff.

Ode to the things I
would not buy, I find
have meaning when they
come from you.

A gift, a trinket,
manifestations of
love, hand to reaching
heart...... heart to
reaching hand ....

LOVE to the things I
would not buy.......

Today I Choose

I choose to put aside the **mourning** papers
I've been interested in them long enough
So today I choose to think about the following:

How many babies were born today?
How many apples fell naturally from trees?
How many hands went up giving glory to God?
How many kisses were the first?
How many smiles melted frowns?
How many hearts beat in sync?

Tomorrow - you get to choose.

Something Lost

From the ashes of churches
torched in history's past
rise seedlings of hope - peeking shyly
finding light.

From the grip of pain's constant pulsing hold
comes the gentle soothing promising
grip of a newborn's hand - clutching only
your index finger.

From the long arduous walk
from the fresh gravesite -
comes the bounding leap over a puddle
... to spare your brand new shoes.

OH! TIME TRAVELER - Though it seems
you've lost more than you've won
you miss more than you enjoy
you cry more than you smile
you hide more than you share
you wish more than you do
you regret more than you strive
            I say to you
 Use that which has been lost, recreate it
          starting new memories....

Sparkle

Every now and then a shiny sparkle dances off the wall

in the darkness of night

barely visible from the corner of your right eye.

But . . you know without a doubt that you saw it.

Convincing a friend during lunch the next day, seems futile,

somehow the encounter just cannot be conveyed.

But it's ok, 'cause I saw it too.

that *sparkle* is the friendship between me and you.

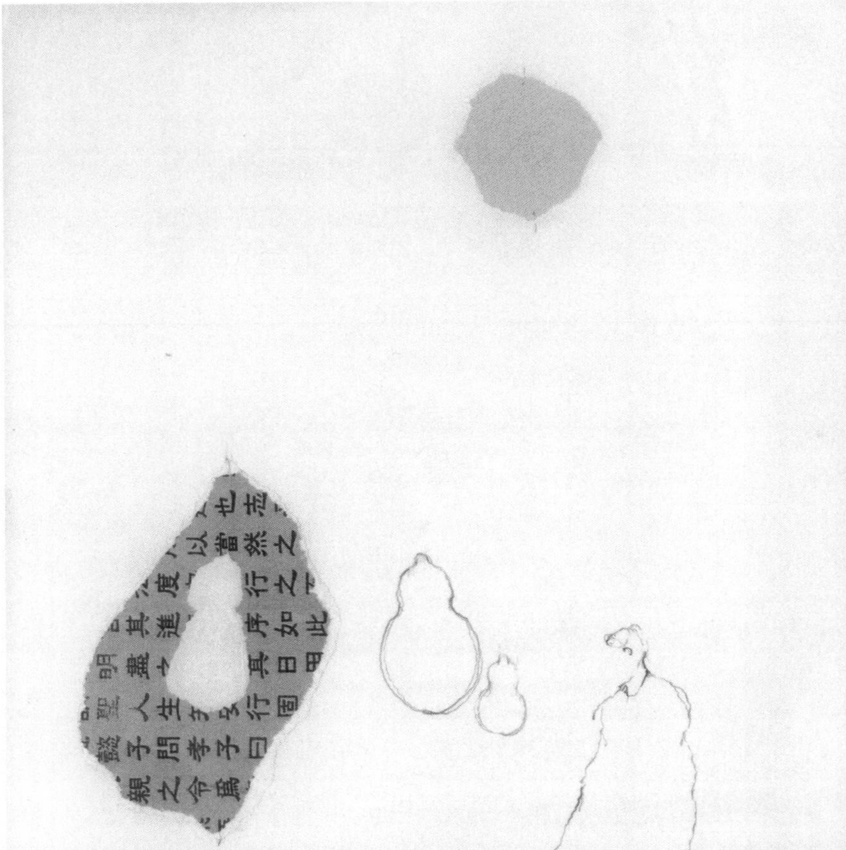

EPISODE NINE

stepping out

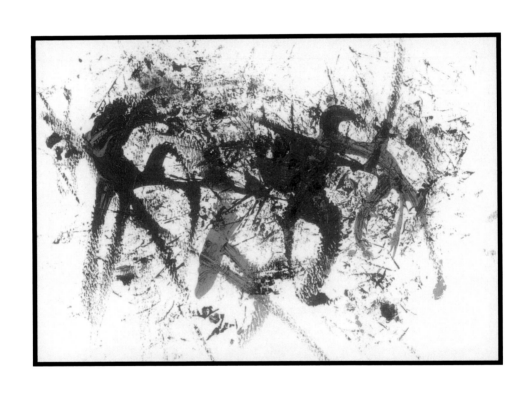

The Shelf

I believed as a child when you placed your most treasured toys on the shelf come evening , that surely, come morning you would reach confidently retrieving their comfort.

I never dreamed of a day the shelf would be bare.

Now, I find myself challenged, replacing my toys with memories, on the shelf of my mind . . . . . . funny, it never needs dusting.

T`was Lead to Believe

That!   the relationship was solid
           no room for questions

That!   the communication was beyond
           one mind but unique

That!   the song was sacred to
           our morning ritual

That!   the sweet sound of my jade
           and gold bangles stirred
           only your energy

That!   the sound of me awaking
           in all its glory meant
           only to you ..that the
           day has cheerfully begun

BUT NO! now that you moved
           downstairs and reside content
           partaking in earlybird activities
           discussing with your new friends
           our private games

           I am left to only realize

That! I am not a finch
That! You are not people

           you discovered the deck outside
           now a variety of birds come to sing
           and visit you several times a day

           To the point now - there is
           no response when I awake
           no song to me when I mimic
           your sound - no chirp chirp
           hi mommybird - anymore -

T`was lead to believe
           that I was a finch and that
           you Tweedledee and Tweedledum
           were my friends-

           So enjoy life with the visiting wild birds ....
           I... will go put on some jazz!

To Myself I Say-

Bass player - you struck
a tone which bound
us together -

The promise - of a life
together began its journey -

Gregory my Sweet - your lips
were the catalyst -
the random pie - we have
shared over time
still tastes freshly baked

Through our trials - our family &
friends we have lost -- together
we stand, arms linked in recovery
To myself I say ... SOLID!

maybe **?**

Sighing winds . . . . . carrying a variety of
tiny seeds in the air . . . . whirling . . . . .
whispering
all around us . . .

So delicately finding their way to the fertile
earth . . . to grow into a tree . . . . .

or maybe?... just some weeds . . .

JUST A THOUGHT

friday a.m. , poverty lined streets , it's garbage pick up day

cans of dreams and hopes line up like a holiday affair
the streets now have meaning

a child's unfinished drawing
a recipe attempt which failed
a half-assed incomplete job application

nevertheless - the cans are inevitably overflowing with rotten
dreams and empty souls.

WHO'D DARE TO PICK IT UP- pile it all together

transport raw desire to the city dump to be soiled and picked on
by disease carrying birds of prey

YET WHEN SATURDAY COMES-
the cans are empty, yearning for their fill - which without
question - will be ample by the week's ending

 ..... who'd dare to pick it up

CONCLUSION

Welcome to my chaos...

as I pretend to sleep, pondering...how a miniscule thought can erupt into a volcanic explosion of questions...unanswerable...

why it seems, that the understanding of life's ever-changing theme...does not teach me how to stand steady...but...trembling...

LOVED ONES GO ELSEWHERE... elsewhere-to-where???... leaving me to rest my spine on THE STRENGTH of palm trees... for graceful swaying support...

THEREFORE THE PAINT SHALL REMAIN WET - ALLOWING ME TO ADJUST MY HANDPRINT IN ACCORDANCE WITH REALITY.

time's changing reality...adjusting ever so slightly...

...welcome...

-Thank you, family, friends and strangers-

THANK YOU GOD